Dec 16

Meet the
MIAMI
DOLPHINS

BY
ZACK BURGESS

NORWOODHOUSE PRESS

CHICAGO, ILLINOIS

NORWOOD HOUSE PRESS

P.O. Box 316598 • Chicago, Illinois 60631
For more information about Norwood House Press please visit our website at
www.norwoodhousepress.com or call 866-565-2900.

Photo Credits:
All photos courtesy of Associated Press, except for the following: Black Book Archives (6, 7, 15, 22 both, 23),
Topps, Inc. (10 both, 11 top & middle, 18), McDonald's Corp. (11 bottom).

Cover Photo: Rick Osentoski/Associated Press

The football memorabilia photographed for this book is part of the authors' collection. The collectibles used
for artistic background purposes in this series were manufactured by many different card companies—
including Bowman, Donruss, Fleer, Leaf, O-Pee-Chee, Pacific, Panini America, Philadelphia Chewing Gum,
Pinnacle, Pro Line, Pro Set, Score, Topps, and Upper Deck—as well as several food brands, including
Crane's, Hostess, Kellogg's, McDonald's and Post.

Designer: Ron Jaffe
Series Editors: Mike Kennedy and Mark Stewart
Project Management: Black Book Partners, LLC.
Editorial Production: Lisa Walsh

LIBRARY OF CONGRESS CATALOGING-IN-PUBLICATION DATA
Names: Burgess, Zack.
Title: Meet the Miami Dolphins / by Zack Burgess.
Description: Chicago, Illinois : Norwood House Press, [2016] | Series: Big
    picture sports | Includes bibliographical references and index. |
    Audience: Grade: K to Grade 3.
Identifiers: LCCN 2015026320| ISBN 9781599537337 (Library Edition : alk.
    paper) | ISBN 9781603578363 (eBook)
Subjects: LCSH: Miami Dolphins (Football team)--Miscellanea--Juvenile
    literature.
Classification: LCC GV956.M47 B87 2016 | DDC 796.332/9409759381--dc23
LC record available at http://lccn.loc.gov/2015026320

288N—072016
Manufactured in the United States of America in North Mankato, Minnesota

CONTENTS

Words in **bold type** are defined on page 24.

The Dolphins love to celebrate great plays.

CALL ME A DOLPHIN

Dolphins are smart and swift. They work together and have fun together. You can say the same things about the Miami Dolphins. Maybe that is why so many fans cheer for them. The "Fins" play exciting football. It is hard to root against them!

The Dolphins played their first season in 1966. In 1972, they didn't lose a single game! No team in the National Football League (NFL) had ever done that. The Dolphins owe much of their success to coach **Don Shula**. They have also had great quarterbacks, including Dan Marino.

Dan Marino was the best passer in team history.

The Dolphins' stadium is a perfect place to watch a game.

BEST SEAT IN THE HOUSE

The Dolphins play in one of the country's best football stadiums. It is often chosen to host the Super Bowl. In recent years, the Dolphins moved hundreds of seats closer to the field. For the 2015 season, they built a roof to protect fans on rainy afternoons.

SHOE BOX

The trading cards on these pages show some of the best Dolphins ever.

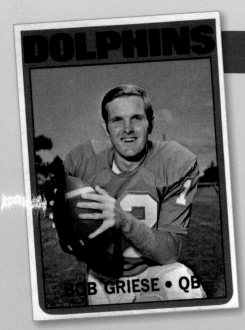

BOB GRIESE

QUARTERBACK · 1967-1980

Bob worked hard off the field to be a great passer. He led the Dolphins to the Super Bowl three years in a row.

LARRY CSONKA

RUNNING BACK · 1968-1974 & 1979

Larry ran like a runaway train. He was the Most Valuable Player in Miami's second Super Bowl victory.

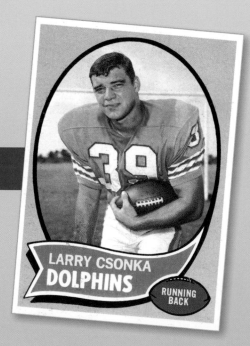

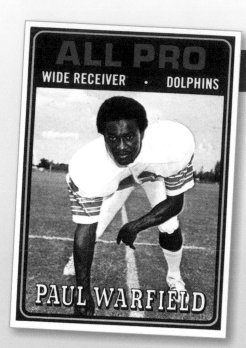

PAUL WARFIELD

RECEIVER · 1970-1974

Paul used his speed to become one of the top receivers of the 1970s. It often took two players to cover him.

MARK DUPER

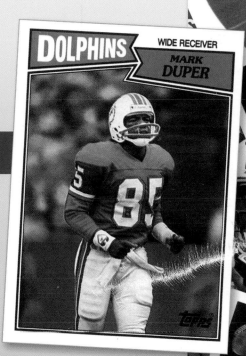

WIDE RECEIVER · 1982-1992

Mark's nickname was "Super Duper." He and Mark Clayton were the NFL's most dangerous pair of receivers.

DAN MARINO

QUARTERBACK · 1983-1999

Dan had a strong arm and threw the ball quickly. He was the first NFL quarterback to pass for 5,000 yards in one season.

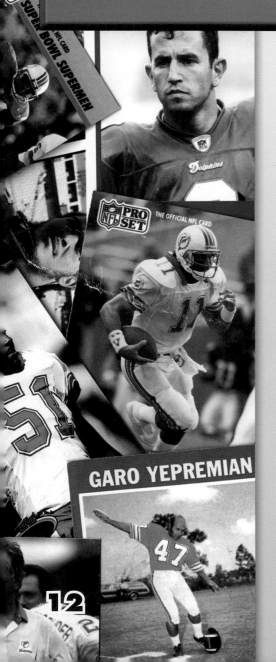

THE BIG PICTURE

Look at the two photos on page 13. Both appear to be the same. But they are not. There are three differences. Can you spot them?

Answers on page 23.

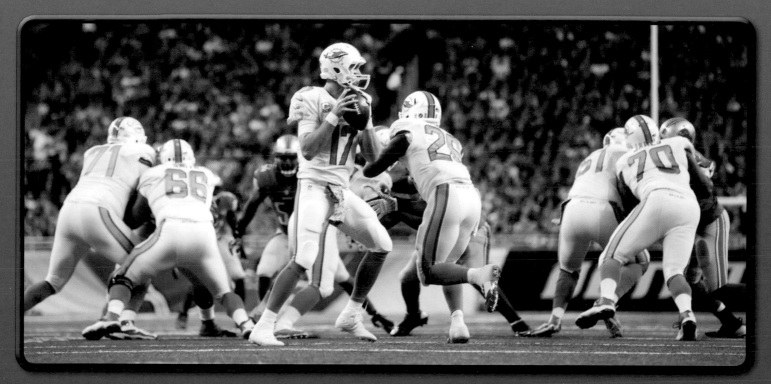

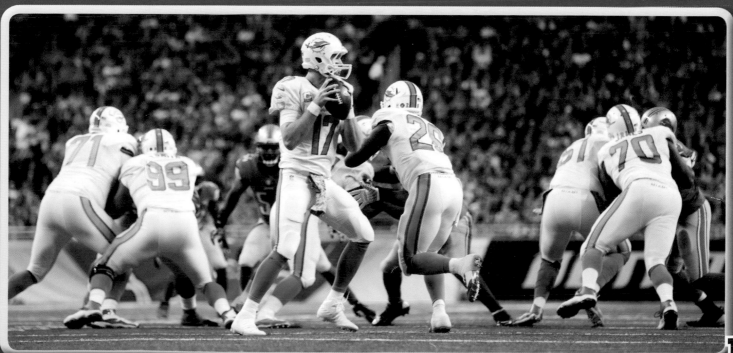

13

TRUE OR FALSE?

Jason Taylor was a star defender. Two of these facts about him are **TRUE**. One is **FALSE**. Do you know which is which?

1 Jason had 131 **quarterback sacks** in 13 seasons for the Dolphins.

2 Jason's mother and father were both tailors.

3 Jason was the NFL Defensive Player of the Year in 2006.

Answer on page 23.

Jason Taylor chases down a quarterback.

Young fans get autographs before a game.

Go Dolphins, Go!

The Dolphins have always had a close bond with their fans. It goes back to the team's first season. Fans in Miami were thrilled to get their own football team. Players like to mingle with them out in public. The team also holds "Fin Fest" events for fans.

ON THE MAP

Here is a look at where five Dolphins were born, along with a fun fact about each.

 1 **ZACH THOMAS • PAMPA, TEXAS**
Zach made the **Pro Bowl** seven times for the Dolphins.

 2 **MERCURY MORRIS • PITTSBURGH, PENNSYLVANIA**
Mercury and Jim Kiick each ran for 1,000 yards in 1972.

 3 **LARRY LITTLE • GROVELAND, GEORGIA**
Larry was voted into the **Hall of Fame** in 1993.

 4 **NICK BUONICONTI • SPRINGFIELD, MASSACHUSETTS**
Nick was the leader of Miami's "No-Name Defense" in the 1970s.

 5 **GARO YEPREMIAN • LARNACA, CYPRUS**
Garo was an **All-Pro** kicker twice for the Dolphins.

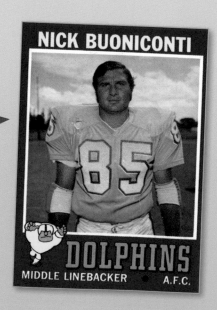

NICK BUONICONTI
85
DOLPHINS
MIDDLE LINEBACKER • A.F.C.

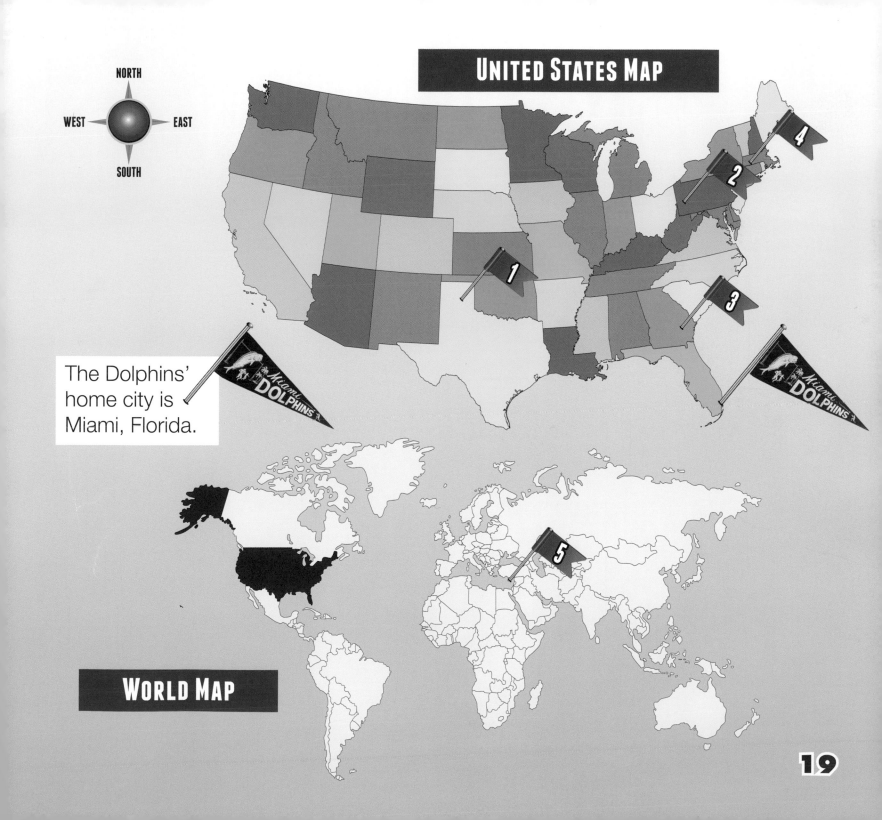

UNITED STATES MAP

NORTH

WEST   EAST

SOUTH

The Dolphins' home city is Miami, Florida.

Miami DOLPHINS

WORLD MAP

HOME AND AWAY

Lamar Miller wears the Dolphins' home uniform.

Football teams wear different uniforms for home and away games. The main colors of the Dolphins are aqua, orange, and white. Aqua is a blue-green color that reminds people of the ocean.

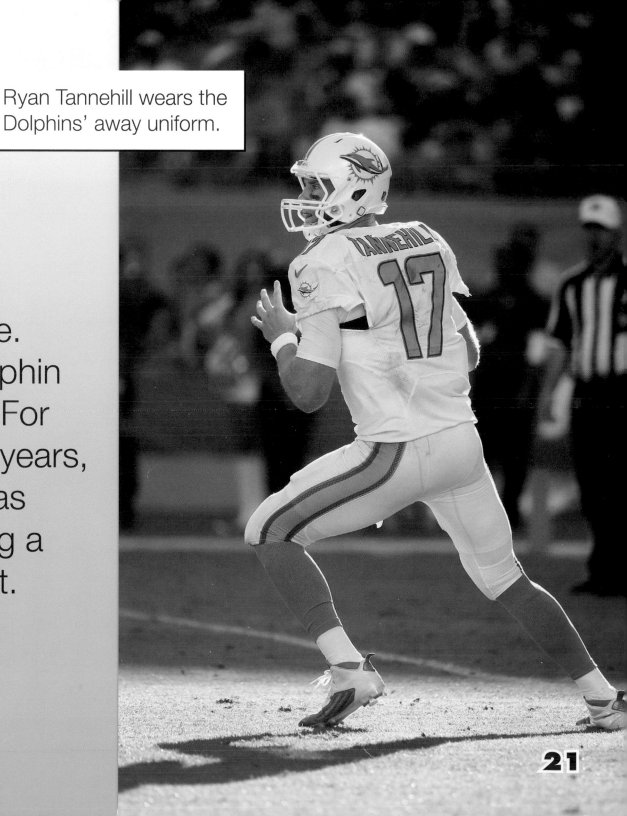

Ryan Tannehill wears the Dolphins' away uniform.

The Dolphins' helmet is white. It shows a dolphin on each side. For more than 40 years, the dolphin was shown wearing a football helmet.

WE WON!

Winning every game over a full season is almost impossible. But the Dolphins did it in 1972. They finished 17–0, including a Super Bowl victory.

Bob Griese and **Earl Morrall** shared the quarterback's job. Morrall was named the league's top player.

RECORD BOOK

These Dolphins set team records.

PASSING YARDS	RECORD
Season: Dan Marino (1984)	5,084
Career: Dan Marino	61,361

RECEIVING YARDS	RECORD
Season: Mark Clayton (1984)	1,389
Career: Mark Duper	8,869

RUSHING TOUCHDOWNS	RECORD
Season: **Ricky Williams** (2002)	16
Career: Larry Csonka	53

ANSWERS FOR THE BIG PICTURE
#66 changed to #99, the stripe on #70's pants changed to orange, and the goal posts disappeared.

ANSWER FOR TRUE AND FALSE
#2 is false. Jason's parents were not tailors.

23

Football Words

All-Pro
An honor given to the best NFL player at each position.

Hall of Fame
The museum in Canton, Ohio, where football's greatest players are honored.

Pro Bowl
The NFL's annual all-star game.

Quarterback Sacks
Tackles of the quarterback that lose yardage.

Index

Photos are on **BOLD** numbered pages.

About the Author

Zack Burgess has been writing about sports for more than 20 years. He has lived all over the country and interviewed lots of All-Pro football players, including Brett Favre, Eddie George, Jerome Bettis, Shannon Sharpe, and Rich Gannon. Zack was the first African American beat writer to cover Major League Baseball when he worked for the *Kansas City Star*.

About the Dolphins

Learn more at these websites:
www.miamidolphins.com • www.profootballhof.com
www.teamspiritextras.com/Overtime/html/dolphins.html